United We Stand
AMERICA RESPONDS TO THE EVENTS OF
September 11, 2001

United We Stand
AMERICA RESPONDS TO THE EVENTS OF
September 11, 2001

HELPING HANDS

A City and a Nation
Lend Their Support at Ground Zero

Marylou Morano Kjelle

CHELSEA HOUSE
PUBLISHERS
A Haights Cross Communications Company

PHILADELPHIA

FRONTIS: The skyline of New York City was forever changed in a few horrible hours on September 11, 2001. But instead of merely inspiring terror in the hearts of Americans, as the terrorists had hoped, the attacks also showed the generous spirit of New Yorkers and Americans as they reached out to help victims and rescue workers alike.

CHELSEA HOUSE PUBLISHERS

EDITOR IN CHIEF Sally Cheney
DIRECTOR OF PRODUCTION Kim Shinners
CREATIVE MANAGER Takeshi Takahashi
MANUFACTURING MANAGER Diann Grasse

STAFF FOR HELPING HANDS

ASSOCIATE EDITOR Benjamin Xavier Kim
PICTURE RESEARCHER Sarah Bloom
PRODUCTION ASSISTANT Jaimie Winkler
COVER AND SERIES DESIGNER Keith Trego
LAYOUT 21st Century Publishing and Communications, Inc.

A Haights Cross Communications ◀ Company

http://www.chelseahouse.com

First Printing

1 3 5 7 9 8 6 4 2

Library of Congress Cataloging-in-Publication Data

Kjelle, Marylou Morano.
   Helping hands : a city and a nation lend their support at ground zero /
Marylou Morano Kjelle.
      p. cm.—(United we stand : America responds to the events of
September 11, 2001)
Includes index.
Summary: Examines the events and aftermath of the September 11, 2001
terrorist attacks, focusing on the aid given to the relief effort by local
citizens and others across the nation and beyond.
   ISBN 0-7910-6959-1 (hardcover)—ISBN 0-7910-7181-2 (pbk.)
  1. September 11 Terrorist Attacks, 2001—Juvenile literature. 2. Disaster
relief—United States—Juvenile literature. 3. Victims of terrorism—
Services for—United States—Juvenile literature. 4. Terrorism—United
States—Juvenile literature. [1. September 11 Terrorist Attacks, 2001.
2. Disaster relief. 3. Terrorism.] I. Title. II. United we stand.
HV6432 .K55 2002
973.931—dc21

                                                      2002008448

TABLE OF
CONTENTS

Foreword

The events of September 11, 2001 will be remembered as one of the most devastating attacks on American soil ever. The terrorist attacks caused not only physical destruction but also shattered America's sense of safety and security, and highlighted the fact that there were many groups in the world that did not embrace the United States and its far-reaching influence. While things have, for the most part, returned to normal, there is still no escaping the demarcation of life before and after September 11—the newest day that will forever live in infamy.

Yet, even in the aftermath of the terror and destruction, one can see some positive effects that have arisen from the attacks. Americans' interest in foreign countries—especially those where Islam is the predominant religion—and U.S. foreign policy has been at an all-time high. The previously mundane occupations of firefighter, police officer and emergency medical worker have taken on a newfound level of respect due to the heroism and selflessness displayed on September 11. The issue of airport security has finally been taken seriously with the implementation of National Guardsmen in airports and undercover air marshals aboard flights.

The books in this series describe how various groups and agencies dealt with the unfolding events of September 11. They also tell the history of these agencies and how they have dealt with other crises in the past, as well as how they are operating in the wake of September 11.

While the rest of us were reeling in shock and horror at what was unfolding before our eyes, there were others whose jobs required that they confront the situation head-on. These are their stories.

Benjamin Xavier Kim
Series Editor

The attacks on the World Trade Center and Pentagon on September 11 were some of the most devastating ever to be carried out on American soil. Many wondered how—and if—the city of New York would ever recover, and how they could help the city in any way they could.

A National Tragedy Unfolds

Tuesday, September 11, 2001 dawned warm and sunny in New York City. Good weather always brings more people out to vote, and it was primary day. New York City residents were selecting the candidates who would run for mayor in the November elections. But on this beautiful day, an unimaginable horror took place: eighteen hijackers armed with box cutters, boarded four separate commercial airliners and launched a terrorist attack that was to become the deadliest day in America's history.

The first plane to hit was American Airlines Flight 11, carrying eighty-one passengers and eleven crew members. It had departed Boston's Logan Airport and was en route to Los Angeles. Soon after takeoff, it was taken over by terrorists, and at 8:45 A.M., was crashed into floors 90 through 100 of the World

Trade Center's north tower. Most people seeing the crash or hearing news of it believed the crash to be an accident—perhaps a private plane that had flown off course and was unable to set itself right.

When the second plane hit the south tower eighteen minutes later, incredulity replaced hope. United Airlines Flight 175, also a Boeing 747, carried fifty-six passengers and nine crew members and crashed into floors 78 through 87 of the second tower. Flight 175 had also departed Logan Airport, and like American Airlines Flight 11, it was also bound for Los Angeles. The second crash left no doubt in anyone's mind—the United States of America was under attack.

On any given day, approximately 50,000 people worked in the World Trade Center and an additional 100,000 visited. The crashing of the planes into the twin towers transformed the area around the World Trade Center into one of unbelievable horror. As thick black smoke poured out of both towers, glass, metal and thousands of pieces of paper—office memos, reports and computer printouts—drifted slowly down to earth. Bodies also fell from the twin towers. Everyday people going about their business at work on an ordinary Tuesday morning suddenly faced death and had to choose between dying in the fire or leaping from the towers.

As the more fortunate World Trade Center employees ran from the buildings, New York City's police, fire and emergency rescue teams, heedless of their own safety, rushed inside to help with the evacuations. The first fire alarms sounded in firehouses as shifts were changing, so the firefighters' response was greater than normal. Known as New York's Bravest, their efforts saved between 20,000 and 25,000 people, but close to 350 of their own would die in the World Trade Center disaster. New York City's Police Department, called New York's Finest, also came out in full force. Twenty-three of their members would be lost.

At 9:43 A.M. America was attacked a third time. A plane crashed into the Pentagon, America's military headquarters located in Arlington, Virginia, a suburb of Washington D.C. Named for its five-sided design, the Pentagon is one of the largest office building in the world and employs close to 24,000 people. American Airlines Flight 77 had departed Washington's Dulles Airport with fifty-eight passengers and a crew of six and was bound for Los Angeles when hijackers took control of the cockpit.

President Bush put America's military on its highest level of alert. A state of emergency was declared for both Washington, D.C. and New York City and fighter planes were ordered to protect both cities. The president called the National Guard to duty and dispatched Navy aircraft carriers and guided missile destroyers to Washington and New York. The United States border with Canada was sealed. The nation's nuclear power plants increased their security. And for the first time in America's history, the Federal Aviation Administration (FAA) grounded all non-military air travel. Airplane departures were cancelled and planes already in the air were turned back or diverted to Canada. Passengers stranded at New York's three airports were walking along streets and highways, luggage in tow, looking for transportation to a hotel room. Amtrak suspended all trains between Washington, D.C. and Boston and Greyhound cancelled all its buses traveling northeastern routes.

Soon after the FAA made its announcement, at 9:49 A.M., a passenger of United Airlines Flight 93 contacted an emergency dispatcher by phone, telling her that plane had been hijacked. Having departed New Jersey's Newark International Airport, the plane carried 38 passengers and a crew of 7, and was en route to San Francisco.

Firefighters arriving at the World Trade Center immediately started for the north tower's upper floors. Survivors recall exhausted firemen charging up the stairs with eighty to one hundred pounds of fire fighting gear on their backs. Their flashlights provided light for people in the stairwells. A firefighter on the 30th floor of the north tower when the second plane hit said, "We were trying to evacuate civilians. The hallways were filled with dust and smoke. The whole building was shaking. We feared it would collapse. I managed to get out of the building a few seconds before it collapsed . . . I don't know what happened to the company. Just me and the lieutenant got out."

Immediately after the towers fell, a 30-block area of downtown Manhattan was closed off. This area, called the Red Zone, included City Hall, Wall Street, state and federal courthouses and government offices. The New York Stock Exchange closed and remained closed for the rest of the week. New York City

"I DON'T THINK MY PARTNER MADE IT"

Immediately after the twin towers collapsed, Chelsea Piers, an entertainment complex in lower Manhattan, was transformed into a center to help victims and rescue workers. The Spirit Cruise Line, docked at Chelsea Piers, converted its pleasure boats into water taxis to carry evacuees to New Jersey. Janice Marie, an employee in the corporate sales department of Spirit Cruises who had seen the second plane strike, was assisting survivors as they waited for transportation. "Most people were calm, almost in shock," she said. The wait to depart the 530-passenger boat was hours long. "It was a hot, sunny day and people were getting sunburned as they waited," Janice said. She gave out bottled water and snacks and tried to get the most traumatized to the front of the line. "People were cooperative, no one objected when we brought someone to the front of the line." With a breaking voice she tells of a dazed businessman who came to the pier covered in ash. "He was wearing a suit, his tie was straight and he was carrying a briefcase," she says. Just before he boarded the boat he turned to Janice and said calmly, "I don't think my partner made it . . . "

Employees and stranded passengers at Newark International Airport as well as other airports had to be directed away from the terminals immediately following the attacks. The Federal Aviation Administration grounded all non-military flights, further complicating matters for air travelers.

public and parochial schools were also closed. Governor George Pataki ordered the New York City primary elections halted, the first time an election had been postponed after voting had started. A new primary date was set for September 25. Most New York City banks closed, but houses of worship opened their doors, inviting the weary and shell-shocked to rest and pray.

As Americans watched the images of destruction in disbelief and horror, surely they must have wondered how the nation—let alone New York City—was going to handle a crisis on such a massive scale, and if anything could ever be the same again. As time went on, it was obvious that recovery was not going to be easy, but fortunately, there were agencies already in place whose goals were to deal with the unthinkable. The resources of these agencies and of the nation would be put to the ultimate test as Americans rushed to provide assistance in any way they could.

Hurricane Floyd was one of the worst natural disasters to strike the U.S. Scenes like this one were common in various cities on the east coast. Though the storm had decreased in severity by the time it approached New York City, it would still cause tremendous problems for the city which needed to be addressed.

2

Past Disasters

Disasters are the result of many things. Humans caused the terrorist attacks of September 11, 2001. Other disasters, hurricanes and earthquakes for example, are natural disasters. Humans do not cause them, nor can humans control them. A plane crash or nuclear power plant meltdown are examples of disasters caused by technological failure. An outbreak of a disease such as anthrax or the flu could cause a biological disaster.

Every large city, including New York City, has had to deal with disasters. In 1996, the Mayor's Office of Emergency Management (OEM) was established. Its purpose is to coordinate the efforts of emergency personnel working on the state and federal level in the event of any type of disaster.

In September 1999, the eastern seaboard of the United States experienced the fury of Hurricane Floyd, a monster of a storm that packed 155-mile-an-hour winds as it blew up the east coast. One of the fiercest hurricanes of the latter part of the twentieth century, Floyd was labeled a category 4. Every state that was in the hurricane's path felt its destruction. Million of people were left without electricity in the south, and parts of North Carolina were under 19 inches of water.

By the time it hit New York City, Floyd had been downgraded to a tropical storm, but its 74-mile-an-hour winds were enough of a threat for New York City's OEM to swing into action. Working in conjunction with federal, state and city agencies, the OEM devised strategies to protect citizens, businesses and infrastructure, to the best of its ability.

Under advisement from the OEM, New York City public schools were closed the first time ever for a hurricane. High winds caused the Port Authority of New York and New Jersey to shut down the upper decks of the Verrazano Narrows Bridge connecting Staten Island and Brooklyn and the George Washington Bridge linking New York and New Jersey. All non-emergency city municipal employees were sent home early. The OEM urged businesses to close and private citizens to remain at home. The United Nations Security Council postponed a meeting and adjourned early.

The projected path of the storm was over the eastern end of New York's Long Island. Governor George Pataki declared a state disaster emergency. Authorities ordered the evacuation of 2000 Long Island residents. The state police were put on alert, and the New York National Guard was on hand to help with the evacuations.

Floyd's effects were felt in New York State by flooding, uprooted trees and wide spread power outages. Residents whose homes were uninhabitable or lost altogether had to turn to agencies such as the American Red Cross for assistance.

The Red Cross was founded in Europe in 1862 as the International Committee of the Red Cross for the purpose of protecting those wounded during war. Using the Red Cross movement as a model, Civil War Nurse Clara Barton began the American Association of the Red Cross (later to be renamed the American National Red Cross) in 1881. In its 120-year history, the American Red Cross has supplemented its wartime work with assistance in disaster relief. Each year, the American Red Cross receives requests for assistance in response to more than 67,000 natural and man-made disasters. The majority of these are house or apartment fires and hurricanes, floods, and earthquakes.

In times of need, the Red Cross provides shelter, food, and health and mental health services to the people affected by the disaster, as well as emergency and rescue workers. The Red Cross also refers those who need supplementary help to other agencies with additional resources.

Another type of assistance needed by the victims of Hurricane Floyd was rental assistance and grants for home repair. These fall under the category of temporary housing assistance and eligibility was determined by the Federal Emergency Management Agency (FEMA). Rental assistance was available if the resident's insurance did not provide for temporary housing assistance.

As Hurricane Floyd illustrates, the quick coordination of federal, state and non-government agencies is needed to

Clara Barton founded the Red Cross in 1881. The organization was first known as the American Association of the Red Cross, based on the European organization known as the International Committee of the Red Cross, which protected the wounded during times of war.

assist victims of any disaster. Never was this coordination more crucial than in the days following the September 11 attacks. In particular, Mayor Rudy Giuliani would prove to be an important figure overseeing the recovery of New York City.

New York Mayor Rudy Giuliani became the symbol of New York's resilience and strength as he led the city throughout the recovery process following the attacks. He became so popular that some even petitioned to re-elect him for another term.

3

Springing to Action

Mayor Rudolph Giuliani was having breakfast at the Peninsula Hotel in midtown Manhattan when the first plane crashed into the north tower. Rushing to the scene, he arrived just as the second plane struck the south tower. Giuliani had less than four months remaining in his term of office. That very day, residents of the five boroughs of New York City were going to the polls in a primary election to begin the process of electing his successor.

After two terms and eight years in office, Giuliani was confident he was leaving New York City in better shape than he had found it when first elected mayor. Crime was down by two-thirds, over six hundred thousand people were off welfare and a good deal of the drug traffic was gone from the city. In his personal life, he was recovering from prostate cancer, a failed marriage and an aborted attempt to run for Senate, an election in which the Republican mayor's opponent would have been First Lady Hillary Rodham Clinton.

Now New York City faced a challenge unparalleled in its history. When Giuliani arrived at the World Trade Center, New York City Police Commissioner Bernard Kerik was already there. The city's command center, established before September 11 on the 23rd floor of 7 World Trade Center, had to be evacuated. Nearly trapped by falling debris when the south tower fell, the mayor and his aides used Engine 24' s firehouse off Houston Street as a makeshift command center. Later the same day, the mayor's center of operations was set up in a police academy on East 20th Street, where it remained for 3 days.

The city was put on high alert. No one knew if more attacks were forthcoming. To protect the city, the Port Authority of New Jersey and New York closed bridges and tunnels in the city's metropolitan area. Train service was halted. The New Jersey Turnpike was closed north of Exit 11, leaving open only the southbound lanes out of New York City. Over-crowded buses, both private and city-owned, were pressed into service to get those who lived in Manhattan home. Commuters by the thousands needing to get to other boroughs crossed the bridges that span the East River on foot. All of New York's ferries and tour companies, including New York Waterways, the Circle Line and Spirit Cruises became water taxis to get people across the Hudson and East Rivers. Private boat owners throughout the area volunteered to transport people out. "Everybody that has a boat in the water is trying to help out," said Captain Norman Littles of the ferry service New York Waterways. Normally, New York Water-ways transports 32,000 commuters a day. On September 11, it estimates it carried 200,000 people. By the evening rush hour, with the exception of lower Manhattan, trains

Many ferry services, such as the Circle Line ferry shown here, helped evacuate people to get them home after all roads and subways were shut down in New York. Many other people had to walk back to their respective homes.

and subways were running close to normal.

More than 9,000 people lived in lower Manhattan near the World Trade Center. Those who lived south of Canal Street were not allowed back into their homes immediately after the attacks. Many relocated to Ferris High School in Jersey City, where a shelter was set up for them. It would be months before those living closest to the twin towers could return home.

Fearing more attacks, parents throughout the New York area rushed to take their children out of school. Some New York City schools prepared to stay open into the evening hours to allow for those parents who might be stuck downtown and unable to pick up their children. Other schools were preparing to keep students overnight in the event they couldn't get home, or there was no home to go to. The six schools nearest the twin towers were evacuated to Staten Island for the day, returning Tuesday evening. When schools re-opened later in the week, six hundred and fifty schoolchildren of P.S. 234, located in the "Red Zone" of Ground Zero, doubled up with students of P.S. 41 on West 11th Street.

To accommodate the thousands of loved ones that descended upon the area hospitals searching for the missing, three thousand volunteers turned 125,000 square feet of space on Pier 94 into a "family center." There, those who were searching could find solace and a measure of comfort as they waited for word. Visitors were served meals and drinks and could speak with a mental health professional and obtain counseling, if they wished.

Throughout the day on September 11, Giuliani remained composed and calm. He walked back and forth between the police academy and Ground Zero. Wearing a hard hat and equipped with a walkie-talkie (as there was no cellular phone service in lower Manhattan), Giuliani continuously urged confused and dazed pedestrians to walk north, towards uptown. Despite the reports of enormous loss of life, including many of his personal friends, he remained focused on the city's reaction to the tragedy. He visited Bellevue and St. Vincent's hospitals, where medical and emergency personnel were awaiting the injured. Later when reflecting back on September 11 and the days following, Giuliani would call it "the most difficult week in the history of New York."

The New York City Fire Department suffered the most losses of any city agency. A total of six hundred firefighters were at the World Trade Center at the time of its collapse. 343 firefighters, including the city's most elite rescue units, were lost. The collapse of the World Trade Center towers was

Members of the New York Fire Department scour through the rubble of Ground Zero. The FDNY were especially driven to search for survivors since they had lost so many firefighters in the attacks.

the worst disaster in fire department history. In addition to the firefighters lost, its highest and second-highest uniformed officers were also killed at the World Trade Center. The first recorded death attributed to the terrorist attacks was that of Father Mychal Judge, a sixty-eight-year-old fire department chaplain who was killed by falling debris as he ministered to the injured. At least thirty New York City fire trucks were crushed beneath the falling towers.

The spirit of New Yorkers remained strong throughout the crisis. "Tomorrow New York is going to be here," Giuliani said. "And we're going to rebuild and we're going to be stronger than we were before . . . I want the people of New York to be an example to the rest of the country, and the rest of the world, that terrorism can't stop us."

The twin towers of the World Trade Center in 1990. Although the towers were originally built and designed to withstand a crash from a jet plane, no one had anticipated the jet fuel causing fires of such high temperatures. The fires eventually caused the metal beams to melt, resulting in the buildings' collapse.

4

Through the Rubble

The twin towers of the World Trade Center had been built to defy hurricanes and high winds, and even the impact of a jumbo jet. But no one anticipated the destruction caused by a commercial jet fully loaded with 20,000 gallons of fuel. Steel melts at 1000 degrees Fahrenheit; at 1500 degrees it becomes soft and malleable. The jet fuel fire, estimated to be 2000 degrees, melted the columns holding the walls and the trusses connecting the concrete floors to the walls. The steel columns buckled outward, allowing the floors to crash straight down one on top of the other in a "pancake configuration." First the south tower, and then the north tower, collapsed in a mushroom-like cloud of dust, ground concrete and ash. Eyewitnesses reported that the buildings appeared to implode inward. The collapse of the twin towers damaged several nearby buildings and resulted in mounds of rubble eight to nine stories high. Cars parked in the vicinity exploded as the fire's heat ignited gas tanks.

The operation immediately after a catastrophe is known as a search-and-rescue operation. The word "rescue" implies there are lives to be saved. Fighting acrid smoke that burned their eyes and made it difficult to breathe, emergency workers by the thousands rushed to the site of the fallen towers and immediately began searching for survivors. On hands and knees they sifted through the rubble with picks and shovels. Some rescuers used their bare hands. They carefully climbed piles of twisted metal, shining their flashlights into chasms searching for signs of life. Many of the rescuers were fire-fighters whose comrades were trapped in the rubble. While New York City firefighters searched for colleagues trapped at Ground Zero, firefighters from surrounding New York State counties as well as other states staffed the city's fire stations and helped perform the duties of those missing or participating in the recovery.

Before noon the Federal Emergency Management Agency's (FEMA) fully activated emergency response teams were coordinating the search-and-rescue operation. FEMA teams consisted of emergency medical technicians, firefighters, paramedics, logistics and communication specialists, struc-tural engineers, chaplains and search and rescue dogs trained to detect the scent of human flesh. The dogs, used to rescuing live humans, began showing signs of depression when they found no one alive. Rescuers would then hide in the rubble and pretend to be rescued to lift the dog's spirits.

3,000 members of the New York National Guard were called out to help search for victims or guard the area around the World Trade Center. New York state police joined them. Rescuers and emergency workers wearing breathing masks struggled against time to find survivors in the rubble.

Several times the search was halted as the sound of a klaxon horn signaled a building was on the verge of collapse. Several buildings were still on fire. Other fires erupted as debris was cleared. Rescuers worked around gas lines ruptured by falling metal and concrete as debris from damaged buildings continued to fall. "This is a very dangerous rescue effort," Mayor Giuliani said. "The men and women who are doing it are literally putting their lives at risk."

Some rescuers kept portable oxygen tanks with them. They contained 30 minutes of oxygen (for normal breathing), but because the work was so demanding, the oxygen lasted only 10 minutes for the rescue workers. Two-way microphones attached to long sticks were poked inside the rubble to detect sounds of life. Infrared imaging cameras were deployed to locate "hot spots"—places were people could still be alive. Small robots were sent to scout out survivors in areas too dangerous for humans. Once it was possible to move around at Ground Zero, rescue workers traveled from one area to another in golf carts.

An estimated 2 million tons of wreckage resulted from the collapse of the Twin Towers. By 2 P.M., the first of many bulldozers arrived and cleared a single lane of Liberty Street so that fire trucks could reach the burning buildings, and smoldering debris. In the days following hundreds of trucks of all kinds lined the West Side Highway as they waited for their turn to enter Ground Zero. Large pieces of metal were loaded onto flatbed trucks by 120-foot cranes. Back-hoes and back-end loaders scraped up smaller pieces of debris, which was hauled away by sanitation trucks. The debris was taken to Staten Island's Fresh Kills landfill. There it was checked by federal agents looking for personal effects of the victims, as well as clues that would provide information about the hijackers.

The bulldozers were joined by a parade of cranes, backhoes and excavators. A demolition company from Bayonne, New

Debris cleared from Ground Zero was eventually brought to the Fresh Kills landfill in Staten Island, NY, where it would be picked through by federal agents to look for clues and personal effects of the victims.

Jersey donated the only operating Caterpillar 345 Excavator. Its concrete pulverizer had a shear on its end to enable it to break through concrete and steel building material.

The mechanical claws of excavation equipment cautiously removed large masses of debris from the top of "the Pile," the mountain of steel and metal that stood several stories high. Acetylene torches and diamond-tipped buzzsaws cut chunks of steel into smaller pieces to make them easier to remove. The heavy equipment scraped off debris layer by layer, inch by inch. After working on a smaller pile for an hour or so, hundreds of rescue workers working shoulder to shoulder sifted through the debris. They formed a bucket brigade to transport rubble to the trucks ready to cart it away. "This cleanup is not going to move at lightening speed," said Will Flower, spokesman for a garbage hauler. "This is going to be methodical and slow—it has to be to ensure all the victims are accounted for and no clues are lost."

Construction in Manhattan came to a stop as all available carpenters, laborers, ironworkers, steamfitters and crane operators were called to help out in the rescue effort and clean up. They were assisted by construction workers and firefighters that came from all across America to lend a hand at Ground Zero. Whenever a body was found, all work stopped as the flag-draped body bag was carried away from the site.

Organization eventually replaced chaos. "Everyone was so focused on finding survivors that at first everything was

Rescuers searching for survivors at the World Trade Center and the Pentagon used everything from their bare hands to the most sophisticated excavation equipment. Handheld tools such as spreaders and cutters pulled apart pieces of debris and cut through chunks of metal. Lift bags were inserted under concrete and pumped with air. As they inflated, pieces of concrete were lifted to allow a rescue worker to see beneath the rubble. More sophisticated hydraulically inflated lifts were used on larger pieces of concrete debris. When there was no danger of a natural gas leak, acetylene torches were used to cut steel and iron into manageable chunks. Diamond-tipped saws were also used for cutting metal. Picks and axes were used to chop and cut through smaller piles. When rescuers were working shoulder to shoulder, they used shovels and rakes to comb through fine rubble, which they loaded into buckets and passed one to the other until the contents were discarded in sanitation trucks.

disorganized and confused," related William Capparelli, a New York City Sanitation Worker who arrived on Tuesday evening to help with the cleanup. Eventually the site was divided into six sections. Contractors experienced in emergency response assigned machinery operators to various tasks.

Rescue workers working in two-person teams accessed a section of rubble, checking for signs of life or air pockets where someone might still be alive. Then they made a determination as to which tools to use to search for survivors. Wearing respirators with filters and goggles and gloves, workers hand-shoveled the ash and dust looking for human remains, body parts and personal effects found near the bodies. Utility workers worked side by side with rescue workers as Consolidated Edison laid 100,000 feet of cable to create a temporary power system for the rescue work.

Whenever a rescue worker thought a noise was heard in the rubble, all activity stopped. One volunteer said, "When they call for silence on the pile . . . it caused me to say a prayer. It meant there was a possibility—a hope that we had found something."

Rescue efforts continued round the clock. Bright stadium lights powered by emergency oil or gas generators the size of tractor trailers illuminated the area. Ground Zero workers went on 12-hour shifts. As the days wore on, deserted office buildings became dormitories where volunteers from out of state slept on the floor. Some volunteers slept in the lobby of the Embassy Suites Hotel in the World Financial Center. Weary rescuers and emergency workers awoke to fresh toothbrushes and hot breakfasts—just two examples of the kindness extended to them by strangers in appreciation for their work.

A heavy rain on Thursday night both helped and hindered the rescue effort. It cleared away much of the dust in the air, but it filled the air cavities under the rubble with water and it

Stadium lights were brought to Ground Zero in order to allow for rescue and recovery efforts through the night. The sheer brightness of the lights could be easily seen from the sky as illustrated in this overhead photo of New York City.

made the piles of debris slippery. "There is an increased hazard . . . because the equipment can slip and people can slip," said John Schuring, an expert on structural design, who also pointed out that the weight of the rain could cause the debris to shift. Workers continued on through the rain wearing ponchos, rain jackets or garbage bags with holes cut out for their arms and heads. The police dogs wore tiny orange rubber boots.

On September 14, three days after the disaster, it was announced that only a limited number of screened volunteers would be allowed at Ground Zero. "We were off duty and couldn't just sit around," said Bill Kiger, a firefighter from Rahway, New Jersey, who was experienced in rescue work in tunnels and collapsed buildings. He ended up helping to carry bags of donated clothing. "Anything we can do is worthwhile," he said.

Only five people were rescued alive from the World Trade Center rubble. The last survivor was found on Wednesday, September 12. As rescue workers raced against time to find people alive, rumors of false rescues circulated the area. "If there's anything disheartening, it's that we have worked hours and hours and haven't found anything," said Thomas Scotto, president of the New York City Detective Endowment Association. When it was no longer likely that anyone else would be rescued alive, the search-and-rescue operation became a search-and-recovery operation. The United States Public Health Service sent medical examiners to help identify the deceased. As dead bodies were found, stores surrounding Ground Zero were pressed into service as temporary morgues.

On Friday, September 14, 2001, President George W. Bush visited Ground Zero. Speaking through a bullhorn he addressed the rescue workers. "Thank you for your hard work. May God bless you now," he said. The workers chanted "USA! USA!" in reply.

On Sunday, September 16, Cardinal Edward Egan, Archbishop of the Diocese of New York, celebrated a mass in honor of those that died, were injured and responded heroically to the disaster at the World Trade Center. He told those who attended he had renamed "Ground Zero." Its new name, Cardinal Egan said, was "Ground Hero."

With 17.5 miles of corridors, six million square feet of office space and 23,000 employees, the Pentagon is the largest office building of the federal government. Built in 1943, the fireproof building had recently been renovated to withstand a bombing.

After Flight 77 crashed into the Pentagon, the report of another plane headed toward Washington, D.C. caused the evacuation of the West Wing of the White House and all federal office buildings. Vice President Cheney and members of the national security staff were taken to a bunker beneath the White House. Congressional leaders were moved to a secure government facility in the Blue Ridge Mountains of Virginia, 75 miles west of Washington, D.C.

Armored vehicles and military police dressed in combat fatigues guarded the streets of Washington, D.C. Sharpshooters were stationed on the roof of the White House and other federal buildings as military helicopters patrolled the skies. All federal government buildings closed, and a quarter of a million government employees headed home for the day. Commuters could only leave the city as all inbound roads, bridges and tunnels were closed. All roads leading to the Pentagon were blocked and mass transit with stops at an underground station at the Pentagon were detoured.

The Department of Defense firefighters located at the Pentagon were the first to respond. Firefighters, police officers, rescue workers, and military personnel from throughout the area soon joined them. Two hundred and forty members of a special urban search and rescue team assisted. Their efforts to reach the site of the crash were complicated by smoke and fire fed by burning jet fuel. The firefighting was also hampered by repeated evacuations due to fear of another attack.

"We were there about 14 hours straight, battling smoke in the dark. But the frustrating thing was we had to keep dropping our gear and running for our lives when we wanted to stay and save other lives," said Andrea Kaiser, a firefighter from Arlington County.

"The area of the Pentagon where the aircraft struck and burned sustained catastrophic damage. Anyone who might have survived the initial impact and collapse could not have survived the fire that followed," read a written report issued by the Defense Department.

FBI agents search outside the Pentagon for clues after one of the hijacked planes crashed into the building. Luckily, the loss of life at the Pentagon was far less than that of the World Trade Center attack, since the plane had crashed into a newly renovated section of the Pentagon where relatively few people had been working.

While members of the FBI searched the roadways and grassy areas around the Pentagon for evidence and pieces of the airplane, rescue workers used a relatively new tool in search and recovery—directional antennas and other radio frequency tracking equipment that could detect signals from buried cell phones, beepers and pagers to locate survivors.

The Pentagon's heliport and many of its sixteen parking lots were over run with ambulances, fire engines and other emergency vehicles as help arrived from surrounding states. Search-and-rescue equipment and dog sniffing units arrived on the scene. One area of the grounds was set up as a field hospital, another as a temporary morgue. Helicopters transported the injured to area hospitals.

For the first time in America's history, Secretary of Health and Human Services Tommy G. Thompson activated nationally a federally coordinated disaster response team. FEMA was deployed to Virginia as well as New York. The federal government made emergency medical supplies available at both sites, and more than three hundred medical and mortuary workers were dispatched to both locations.

The United States Army suffered the largest losses in the Pentagon crash, with twenty-one officers and fifty-three civilians killed. Still, many lives were spared at the Pentagon on September 11 because the plane crashed into a newly renovated area of the building's west wing where offices had not yet been occupied. The plane crashed into the Pentagon's five concentric rings, but only a portion of the outermost corridor, known as the E ring, completely collapsed

President Bush visited the Pentagon, saying "coming here makes me sad on the one hand. It also makes me angry." The president shook hands with dozens of search and rescue workers and praised the firefighters and emergency workers for their hard work.

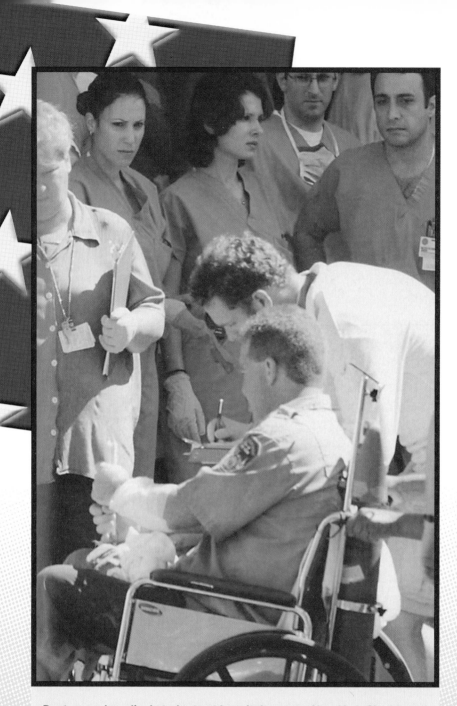

Doctors and medical students at hospitals across New York City braced for a flood of injuries, but soon it was all too apparent that after the first wave of victims requiring medical attention, there would be few survivors from the World Trade Center collapse.

5

Attending to the Wounded

Doctors working at hospitals throughout New York City raced to Ground Zero. Expecting to treat thousands of injured, volunteers constructed makeshift stretchers using two by fours and plywood. As the hours wore on, medical personnel came to the sad conclusion that few people would be rescued alive. One of the first triage (a method of assessing the severity of the wounded) centers to spring up was at a television studio lot at Chelsea Piers. Several triage centers sprung up right at Ground Zero. Firefighters and rescue workers injured by falling debris or sustaining sprained ankles and other non-life threatening injuries were treated as needed. "We've all got surgical training, but the most we've done is give eye drops to firemen," said one volunteer, Dr. James Snyder.

Because a large number of injured were expected, all New York metropolitan area hospitals went on full disaster alert status. When a hospital goes on full alert, elective surgery is cancelled, all patients that could be are discharged, additional staff is called in, and staff members currently at home are put on a standby status. The use of emergency vehicles such as rescue squads and ambulances were reserved for true emergencies. Many hospitals and communities in New York, New Jersey and Connecticut sent emergency vehicles to Ground Zero.

The state of New Jersey immediately implemented its pre-planned emergency response. After the 1993 bombing of the World Trade Center, New York and New Jersey entered into a "Memorandum of Understanding" whereby each state would share its resources with the other in the event of a catastrophe. Now both states went into disaster mode and began implementing the plan for dealing with a disaster of this magnitude.

Hundreds of ambulances from neighboring states waited to be called to Ground Zero from Giants Stadium in New Jersey's Meadowlands. New Jersey set up a state command center at Liberty State Park, part of the Statue of Liberty tourist area, for Emergency Management workers who wanted to help in New York City. The Holland Tunnel was closed to all but emergency vehicles. Jersey City Medical Center, across the Hudson River from New York, sent an ambulance to Ground Zero that was equipped to serve as a portable operating room. New York Waterways, a commuter ferry service, put many of its twenty-four boats into service as floating ambulances from lower Manhattan to New Jersey, Queens and Brooklyn.

Triage centers were set up wherever there was the expectation of many injured. Those who felt they had been exposed to asbestos and other hazardous material were first decontaminated with a spray of water. Using the standard triage color code, their injuries were assessed. Patients who were minimally injured were marked with a green tag while the slightly injured received a yellow tag. Those with life-threatening injuries were marked with red tags and the dead with black tags. Some patients died before they could be transported to a hospital. Others were suffering from burns covering various parts of their bodies. Most survivors did not have injuries serious enough for hospital admission and decided they would see their own doctor or visit a hospital in their community. Emergency rooms dealt mainly with breathing problems and sprained and broken bones and irritated eyes and throats. Emergency rooms were also treating people for acute stress disorder, anxiety chest pain and anger.

Twelve hospitals in New York and New Jersey geared up to accept the injured. The most severe cases were sent to New York hospitals, the less injured to New Jersey. St. Vincent's and Bellevue, the two closest hospitals to the World Trade Center, began attending to arriving patients immediately. As of mid-afternoon on the day of the attack, 950 people had been admitted to hospitals; 150 were in critical condition.

A group of 125 surgeons attending a medical conference at the Meadowlands in New Jersey volunteered to help wherever needed. Some were taken directly to Ground Zero while others staffed triage centers. The federal government sent two navy hospital ships—the *John F. Kennedy* and the *George Washington*—to assist with the injured.

Open-air triage centers were set up to be available to people as they walked off the bridges. Commuters arriving back in New Jersey after taking ferries and buses were met by emergency service workers and Red Cross volunteers who offered medical exams. Most people were what medical professional call "the walking wounded," who had treatable injuries like cuts and abrasions. Many were complaining of difficulty breathing. The more seriously injured were taken by ambulance to local hospitals. An estimated 4500 people received medical treatment in some capacity on September 11.

Within hours of the World Trade Center collapse, thousands of relatives and friends of the missing began to congregate in lower Manhattan. They stood for hours in lines that extended for city blocks to check hospital admission rosters. Volunteers shuttled people from hospital to hospital in search of missing loved ones whom might be unconscious or disoriented and unable to identify themselves. Photographs of the missing along with information about them were posted everywhere in New York City. Family members and friends were encouraged to register missing loved ones with either the National Crime Information Center or the Red Cross. In doing so, they filled out a seven-page questionnaire asking for details about the missing person's blood type, hairstyle, scars or tattoos or other distinguishing marks. Volunteers helped family members fill out the reports.

Businesses with offices in the World Trade Center sent surviving employees to area hospitals for current survivor lists. They did what they could to help families find missing employees. Special phone lines were set up for those not able to find a family member.

Walk-in counseling centers sprung up all over Manhattan—at the Armory, the New School and on Pier 94. In the aftermath of the tragedy, hospitals and community organizations set up crisis centers, grief counseling centers and hotlines. The families of victims, doctors and rescue workers were able to receive counseling. St. Paul's Chapel, a block away from the World Trade Center, ministered to rescue workers. Schools called in crisis counselors to speak to students about the disasters. Many who survived the World Trade Center collapse were experiencing survivor's guilt—intense feelings of guilt for being alive and surviving the disaster when friends and co-workers did not.

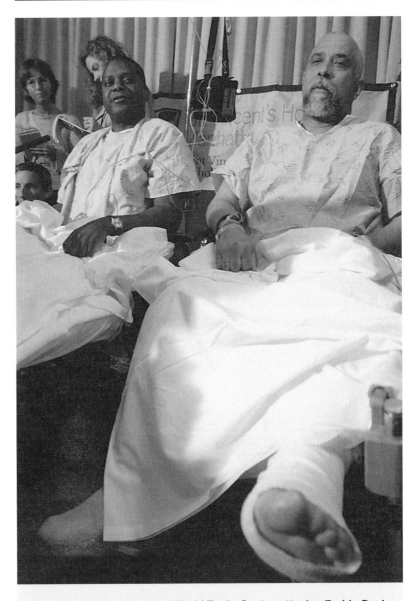

Two lucky survivors of the World Trade Center attacks, Feride Paul (left) and Arturo Griffith, tell their stories at a press conference on September 14, 2001. Paul broke his ankle while running down the stairs in his building near the World Trade Center, while Griffith broke his knee after being in an elevator in the World Trade Center when it was hit.

Many AT&T employees volunteered to make sandwiches for rescue workers at Ground Zero. Here, Lloyd Butler assembles sandwiches at the Salvation Army camp in Pittstown, New Jersey.

6

Outpouring from the Nation

One day soon after the Pentagon crash an Air Force major stopped for a muffin at a coffee shop on his way to work. "I'll ring you up," the owner said, "but you don't have to pay." A woman had come in earlier that morning and had given the owner a handful of money. "Pay the bill of any soldier that walks through the door today," she told him. The woman had lost a family member at the Pentagon. Yet, instead of mourning her loss, she was buying muffins for uniformed servicemen.

After the terrorist attacks at the World Trade Center and the Pentagon, Americans came together as never before. Collectively they were saddened, grief-stricken and angry at what had happened to their country and fellow citizens. They wanted—and needed—to be able to express their emotions in constructive and positive ways. As one volunteer who served meals to workers at Ground Zero said, "I needed to do something. I couldn't stay home and cry and be angry. I needed a constructive way to deal with my emotions."

From the Atlantic Ocean to the Pacific, from Canada to Mexico, American citizens mobilized to show support for the victims of the National Tragedy. In ways large and small, Americans of all ages demonstrated that the true spirit of America is one of compassion and concern. Here is a sampling of the kindness shown by American citizens in the wake of September 11, 2001.

Workers from Long Island Hospital and Brooklyn Hospital Center met survivors of the World Trade Center as they walked over the Brooklyn Bridge and offered them fruit juice and water. Survivors and family members of the Oklahoma City bombing traveled to New York and the Pentagon in support of victims and their families. At Union Square in New York City, two miles from Ground Zero, family members and friends of the missing and dead erected a shrine of remembrance. Schoolchildren throughout the country sent cards, notes and drawings to the rescue workers at both the World Trade Center and the Pentagon, thanking them for their efforts.

The lines to donate blood stretched around buildings in the first days after the attacks. Thousands of pints of blood were collected. Employees of American Airlines, United Airlines and U.S. Airways came together to donate blood en masse and in uniform. Harrah's Casino in Atlantic City, New Jersey had an employee blood drive scheduled; because of the attacks, it was opened to the public. It drew hundreds of donors.

Rev. Joseph A. O'Hare, President of Fordham University in the Bronx, New York, set up a scholarship program whereby the children of Fordham graduates who were victims of the terrorist attacks can attend Fordham at no charge.

Yankees manager Joe Torre wears a commemorative baseball cap while embracing Mayor Giuliani. In the weeks following the September 11 attacks, many showed their solidarity with the firefighters and police officers of New York with hats, T-shirts, and other pieces of clothing.

Large corporations and private foundations pledged money, products and services to help the victims. The United Way of New York City and the New York Community Trust set up the September 11 Fund to help the victims. Also set up were the 911 Firefighters Relief Fund, and a fund through the American Red Cross and many other funds. The New York Yankees pledged $1 million dollars to a fund for families of police officers and firefighters affected by the September 11 disasters.

A team of doctors and nurses drove from Kentucky with

medical supplies for those injured at Ground Zero. Friends and neighbors of the families of the missing, prepared meals, purchased groceries and helped out monetarily. Boy Scout troops did yard work and cut lawns while families searched for missing loved ones. Clergy members of all faiths stationed themselves in public schools in the days immediately following September 11 so that they were readily available to speak with or counsel any student having difficulty coping with the tragedy. And Financial Planning Associations urged their members to work for the families of victims free of charge.

Thousands of pairs of socks, gloves, underwear, masks, toothbrushes, bottles of painkillers, bottled water and other needed items appeared by the truckload, donated by churches and civic organizations throughout the country to rescue workers at both disaster sites in New York and Washington, D.C. The manager of a sporting goods store on Broadway sheltered people in the store during the twin towers' collapse. As they were leaving, he handed out boots, swimmer's goggles and wet tee-shirts for their faces. Following the attacks, chiropractors, podiatrists and message therapists converged upon the emergency workers and rescue workers at Ground Zero, offering back rubs, messages, and foot care. Families of the victims were offered massages. The Yankees also offered Yankees Stadium as a place where rescue workers could shower and sleep.

Volunteers from AT&T's Basking Ridge, New Jersey's location traveled to the Salvation Army building in lower Manhattan to make 5000 sandwiches for the workers at New York's Ground Zero. In the days immediately following September 11, the Salvation Army was providing 10,000 meals a day to rescue workers and victim's families.

Area restaurants supplied free meals. Students from Manhattan's culinary schools and chefs from well known New York restaurants teamed up to offer "Chefs With Spirit" and fed 15,000 people a day on a Spirit pleasure ship docked at Chelsea Piers. One of the ship's decks was outfitted with pillows and blankets so rescue workers could take naps. The Juilliard School of Music arranged for a quartet of musicians to play for families of victims awaiting word on loved ones at an Armory in Manhattan. A band which is part of the National Association for the Prevention of Starvation traveled to New York City to play "America the Beautiful" and other hymns for the rescue workers and families in mourning. Traveling from fire station to fire station, they marched for eight hours trying to lift the spirits of the city.

Students of all grades throughout the nation held car washes, bake sales and sold lemonade on street corners to raise money for families of victims. As word spread of the numbers of public servants lost, tributes of flowers, food, cards and balloons appeared at police stations and firehouses throughout the city. Senior citizen residents of Rest Haven Nursing Home in Ohio, many in their eighties, made flag pins and sold them for $1 each. They raised over $4000 for the Red Cross.

The President of the Manhattan chapter of the American Society for the Prevention of Cruelty to Animals (ASPCA), Larry Hawk started a hot line for those who wanted to help the animals whose owners lived near Ground Zero and could not return home. He also arranged for law enforcement agents to accompany residents back to their homes so they could retrieve their pets. Two hundred pets were rescued. Mr. Hawk also arranged for over 300 injured pets to be treated at Medical Command Centers. Amazingly, all of this work on behalf of animals was done after being notified that his sister, Kathy Nicosia a flight attendant for American Airlines, had been working on Flight 11. Additionally, volunteer veterinarians looked after the canine rescue teams. Animal lovers everywhere donated dog food, bowls, cages, chew toys and blankets.

Two Chicago firefighters collect donations for a memorial fund toward aiding families of New York firefighters who died in the World Trade Center attacks. Firefighters everywhere, even in other countries, expressed their sympathy and sorrow with their fallen brethren in New York.

Fearing that many parents would be unable to return home at their normal hour, schools within commuting distance of the World Trade Center and Pentagon made sure all students had someone at home to greet them after school on September 11. New Jersey municipalities provided relatives of victims free transportation to New York City to search for loved ones or report them missing. And after subway service was shut down in New York City, hundreds of thousands of people had to make their way out of Manhattan on ferries or buses. Motorists offered rides to total strangers stranded on highways.

Firefighters of Ladder No. 8 in Detroit held a fire boot collection at street intersections in downtown Detroit and received $28,000 in donations for the families of the fire-fighters who died at Ground Zero. Almost seven months after September 11, a New York City fire truck that had been damaged in the attack was put back into service. Members of the Greater New York Automobile Association donated the money to have it repaired.

Matthew Harris and Eddie Perryman, two technicians who recover and process human tissue for the University of Texas Southwestern Medical Center at Dallas, drove 70 square feet of human skin to Washington, D.C. for the burn victims of the Pentagon attack.

Even the internet allowed for people to come together and assist in rescue and recovery efforts. An e-mail organizing a candle light vigil in support of the victims on the Friday evening after the attacks circulated around the world. E-mail networks worked to locate the missing.

America's outpouring of love and generosity for the families of victims who died at the World Trade Center and the Pentagon, and those who were working at both sites, did more than help America come to terms with the events of September 11, 2001. They turned America into a nation of healing.

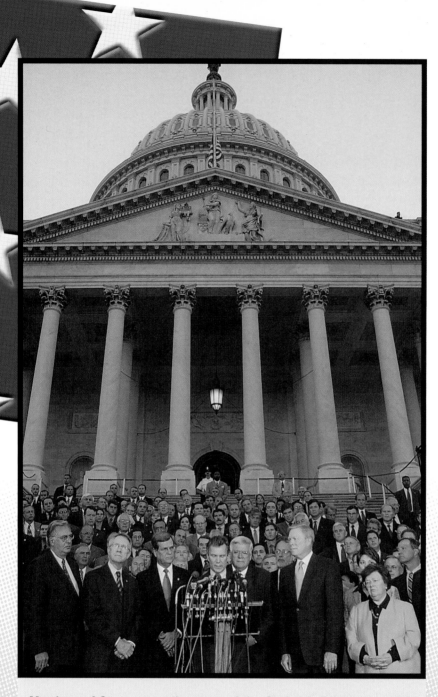

Members of Congress on the steps of the Capitol building show their unity during the evening of September 11, 2001. For a time, all partisan bickering was put aside as Americans of every political leaning came together in sorrow and sympathy.

7

United
We Stand

More than 2900 Americans died in the four terrorist attacks of September 11. This number is almost half that killed during the Revolutionary War and more than the number of lives lost in the attack on Pearl Harbor. Foreign aggression on American soil has been rare. Besides Pearl Harbor, it has only happened twice— during the War of 1812, and in 1846, during the Mexican-American War. Prior to September 11, 2001, the deadliest attack on America was committed by an American. On April 19, 1995, Timothy McVeigh detonated a truck bomb at the Alfred P. Murrah building in Oklahoma City, killing 168 people and injuring over 500.

The events of September 11, 2001 provided the first presidential crisis for George W. Bush, who had been in office less than nine months when they occurred. Inaugurated under a suspicion of voter irregularities, Bush rose to the challenge of the terrorist attacks and emerged a strong and confident leader. The lawmakers and leaders of both the Democratic and Republican parties pledged support to the president and demonstrated their solidarity by singing "God Bless America" on the steps of the capitol building the evening of the attacks. The lawmakers voted to declare Friday, September 14, 2001 a day of unity and mourning.

"We literally and figuratively stand shoulder to shoulder," said Senator Tom Daschle of South Dakota, the House Minority Leader.

In subsequent days, Congress approved a bill allocating $40 billion for disaster relief.

Th American public took up the banner of unity and patriotism in the wake of September 11, 2001. While flags flew at half-mast throughout Washington, D.C., they flew boldly and brightly everywhere else. Store shelves were depleted of American flags as proud citizens displayed them on homes, businesses, cars and street posts. Patriotism increased to a level not seen since the Gulf War ten years earlier. Across the nation, military recruitment offices reported a jump in the number of phone call and walk-in inquiries. President Bush signed an order activating military reservists assigned to port operations, medical support, engineering support and homeland defense. Within days 13,000 Air Force; 10,000 Army; 3000 Navy; 7500 Marines; and 2000 Coast Guard reservists were called up for duty.

Americans honored the victims of the terrorist attacks in other ways. Throughout September, interfaith religious services, moments of silence, memorial and healing services, special prayer services and candlelight vigils were held. Houses of worship were packed as Americans sought to make sense of the tragedy. Clergy members stressed the prevalence of good over evil and the importance of living in the moment. President Bush led the country in prayer at a national prayer service in Washington on September 14. Religious leaders of all faiths took part.

Yet, as America moved towards solidarity and healing it also moved towards retribution. "We will make no distinction

A candlelight vigil on Union Square in New York City was just one of the many memorials that sprang up around the city. Even before the construction of a viewing platform at the site, visitors from all over the world congregated to Ground Zero in the months following the attacks.

between those who committed these acts and those who harbor them . . . Our country is strong. Terrorist attacks can shake the foundations of our biggest buildings, but they cannot touch the foundation of America," said the President. On October 6, 2001, after the Taliban government of Afghanistan refused to give up Osama bin Laden and his terrorist network, America retaliated for the September 11, 2001 attacks with a military strike.

"We will rally the world. We will be patient. We'll be focused, and we will be steadfast in our determination. This battle will take time and resolve, but make no mistake about it, we will win," declared President Bush.

On March 11, 2002, the six-month anniversary of the attacks, memorial services and moments of silence were observed throughout the country for those who had died. Where the World Trade Center had once been, twin beams of blue light were lit into the sky every night for a month after the anniversary date. And on a nearby wooden wall of remembrance were words Rudolph Giuliani, now a private citizen, had written a few weeks earlier: "We will always remember what you did here and you, our heroes, to save America. God bless you."

http://www.nysemo.state.ny.us
   [New York State Office of Emergency Management]

http://www.defenselink.mil
   [The United States Department of Defense]

The American Red Cross
P.O. Box 37243
Washington, DC 20013
http://www.redcross.org
info@usa.redcross.org
(800) 797-8022

Federal Emergency Management Agency (FEMA)
500 C Street S.W.
Washington, DC 20472
http://www.fema.gov

Mercy Corps
3015 SW First, Dept W
Portland, OR 97201
(800) 852-2100
http://www.mercycorps.org

New York Firefighters 9-11 Disaster Relief Fund
P.O. Box 65858
Washington, DC 20035-5858
http://www.helping.org/wtc/laff/adp

New York Police and Fire Widows' and Children's Benefit Fund
General Post Office
P.O. Box 26837
New York, NY 10087-6837
http://www.nypfwc.org

The Salvation Army
P.O. Box C635
West Nyack, NY 10994-1739
(800) 725-2769
http://www.salvationarmy.org

United Way of America
701 North Fairfax Street
Alexandria, VA 22314
(703) 836-7112
http://www.unitedway.org

Canfield, Jack, Mark Victor Handen, Matthew E. Adams.
   Chicken Soup for the Soul of America. Deerfield Beach, FL:
   Health Communications, 2002.

Comb, Cynthia. *Terrorism in the Twenty-First Century*.
   Philadelphia: Running Press, 1999.

Landau, Elaine. *Osama bin Laden: A War Against the West*.
   Brookfield, CT: Twenty-first Century Books, 2002.

Marcovitz, Hal. *The Oklahoma City Bombing*. Philadelphia:
   Chelsea House, 2002.

Alter, Johnathan. "Grits, Guts and Rudy Giuliani." *Newsweek*, September 24, 2001.

Barron, James. "Cardinal Egan Leads Prayers for Victims, and Applause for Rescuers." *The New York Times*, September 17, 2001.

Bush, George W. Transcript of televised speech, September 11, 2001.

Fritsch, Jane. "Rescue Workers Rush In, but Many Do Not Return." *The New York Times*, September 12, 2001.

Gibbs, Nancy. "Life on the Home Front." *Time*, October 1, 2001.

Gibbs, Nancy. "Mourning in America." *Time*, September 16, 2001.

Gillespie, Angus Kress: *Twin Towers: The Life of New York City's World Trade Center*. New Brunswick: Rutgers University Press, 1999.

Hassell, John. "Images Fixed Forever." *The Star Ledger*, September 12, 2001.

Highsmith, Carol M. *World Trade Center: Tribute and Remembrance*. New York: Crescent Books, 2001.

Kennedy, Randy. "With City Transit Shut Down, New Yorkers Take to Eerily Empty Streets." *The New York Times*, September 12, 2001.

McShane, Larry. "Bush Visits Devastation as Nation Unites in Grief." *The Courier News*, September 15, 2001.

Meyers, Steven Lee and Elizabeth Becker, "Defense Department Says 126 Are Missing, Raising Total of Crash Victims to 190." *The New York Times*, September 14, 2001.

Mitchell, Alison and Richard L. Berke. "Differences Are Put Aside as Lawmakers Reconvene." *The New York Times*, September 13, 2001.

Murray, Brian T. and Ron Marsico. "Resignation Spans A River." *The Star Ledger*, September 15, 2001.

New York Magazine Editors. *September 11, 2001: A Record of Tragedy, Heroism and Hope.* New York: Abrahms, 2001.

Raum, Tom. "Pentagon Prevails." *The Courier News,* September 12, 2001.

Sachs, Susan. "Heart Rending Discoveries as Digging Continues in Lower Manhattan." *The New York Times,* September 15, 2001.

Sachs, Susan. "A Delicate Removal of Debris, With Monstrous Machines and Gloved Hands." *The New York Times,* September 14, 2001.

Smith, Dennis. *Report from Ground Zero: The Story of the Rescue Efforts at the World Trade Center.* New York: Viking, 2002.

Steinhauser, Jennifer. "As Remnants Collapse, Workers Run for Cover." *The New York Times,* September 13, 2001.

Sullivan, Robert (Ed). *One Nation: America Remembers September 11, 2001.* New York: Little Brown and Company, 2001.

Thomas, Evan. "Horrors and Heroes of a Day that Changed America." *Newsweek,* December 31, 2001.

Waldman, Jackie (Ed). *America, September 11, 2001: The Courage to Give.* Berkeley: Contari Press, 2001.

Wubbels, Lance. *September 11, 2001: A Time for Heroes.* Shippensburg: Treasure House, 2001.

MARYLOU MORANO KJELLE is a freelance writer and photojournalist who lives and works in central New Jersey. She is a regular contributor to several local newspapers and online publications and writes a column for the *Westfield Ledger/Times of Scotch Plains-Fanwood* called the "Children's Book Nook," where she reviews children's books and writes about the love of reading. She is also the author of *The Waco Siege*, a book in Chelsea House's GREAT DISASTERS: REFORMS, AND RAMIFICATIONS series.